Muslim By Birth, CHRISTIAN BY FAITH

Sam Abu "J"

Copyright © 2013 by Sam Abu "J"

Muslim By Birth, CHRISTIAN BY FAITH
by Sam Abu "J"

Printed in the United States of America

ISBN 9781626979451

All rights reserved solely by the author. The author guarantees all contents are original and do not infringe upon the legal rights of any other person or work. No part of this book may be reproduced in any form without the permission of the author. The views expressed in this book are not necessarily those of the publisher.

Unless otherwise indicated, Bible quotations are taken from The New Living Translation of the Bible. Copyright © 1996, 2004 by Tyndale House Publishers.

Source of verses from the Quran:
Title: AL-QUR'AN
Author: Muhammad Farooq-i-Azam Malik
Copyright: 1997 The Institute of Islamic Knowledge, Houston, TX

www.xulonpress.com

Table of Contents

Chapter

1. Born Muslim 9
2. Moving On...God At Work! 15
3. Wedding Bells 19
4. Life Was Changing Fast 23
5. One September Day! 26
6. Blue-Haired Church Ladies 34
7. A Sunday Morning Church Service 38
8. Meeting The Preacher Man 40
9. "Born Again"...Now What? 45
10. Tough Questions! 49
11. World Religions 54

      Atheists & Agnostics............................55

    Eastern Religions 58

12. The Judeo-Christian Faith 60

13. But Is The Bible Reliable? 72

14. More On How The Bible Came To Be 77

15. Early Opposition Against Jesus 80

16. Faith Is The Only Way 82

17. Islam & Christianity...Let's Compare! 84

18. What Does The Quran Say About Jesus? 92

19. The Bible Is Not Corrupt...Says The Quran 105

20. Putting It All Together 110

21. Now What? Tell My Family? Be Disowned? 114

Dedication

First and foremost, I wrote this book to honor and serve my Lord and Savior, Jesus Christ. If you are a Christian, this needs no explanation. If you are not, I pray that by reading this book, you will understand why dedicating a book to the Lord is hardly worthy of what He has done.

Second, I dedicate this book to my wife, Jessica, and our three children, whom I know were put in my life by the Lord. I also dedicate this book to my beloved pastor, David Jeremiah. Dr. Jeremiah is a humble servant of the Lord. Although his ministry has worldwide reach, he took the time to minister to me, a Palestinian-born American who wanted to know who this Jesus is. Finally, I dedicate this book to my parents and my four siblings. As I write this, they have yet to accept Jesus. I pray that someday they will seek and find the truth.

Chapter 1

Born Muslim

Thank you for taking the time to read this book. I hope it blesses your life. If you are skeptical about Christ, I hope that this walk through my life, my doubts, my fears and my conversion will open your heart and mind to the truth. If you are already a follower of Christ, I hope this book will inspire you to share your faith and equip you to do it in a meaningful and constructive way.

I was born to Muslim parents on the West Bank — Palestine, in the town of Ramallah. According to Islam, that made me Muslim by birth. Yes, in Islam, if your parents are Muslim, you are Muslim. In fact, my birth certificate states RELIGION: MUSLIM. It is especially difficult for Palestinians to convert for obvious reasons. They have been under Jewish occupation for decades and for someone to proclaim the Jew of all Jews (Jesus) as their Lord and Savior just doesn't go over well. The opposite is true of Christianity—you cannot be "born" Christian. There was only one person ever born Christian—Jesus Christ himself. Each person must choose Jesus as their personal Lord and Savior. That's right, even the children of great preachers like Billy Graham have to choose to be Christians. Furthermore, once a person *truly* accepts Christ by faith, their sins are entirely forgiven and their eternal salvation cannot be revoked or cancelled. That's God's promise and He always keeps His promises.

I was three years old when my family immigrated to the United States. My parents were both in their forties and had spent a lifetime living as moderate, everyday Muslims in the West Bank. Both of my parents were school teachers. I am the youngest of five siblings—one brother and three sisters. I don't remember my three years living in Palestine, but we did go back for a visit when I was about eight years old.

Those memories are ingrained in my mind. I saw Israeli tanks rolling through the old villages. Tension was always thick and hatred was the mood. My family made no attempt to hide their feelings for the "occupiers". In fact, they wanted me to understand how bad these people were and how they stole our land. I also recall how I did not fit in with the local kids. They picked on me because I was the "rich kid" coming back from America to visit the poor. In America, my family was hardly rich, but over there—it was a different story. I have yet to return for another visit.

Arriving in America, we spent the first ten years living in a lower middle class town of Warren, Ohio; about two hours south of Cleveland. My father bought a convenience store, as did his brothers who came to the same town before him. Yes, we were your typical Arabs. Actually, that generation probably created the Arab stereotypes we have today.

We were a Muslim family, but very moderate. We never went to Mosque. I don't recall seeing my parents praying much (if ever) and we didn't read or study the Quran. I know we had a Quran in our house, but it was never opened. However, my parents would occasionally mention some basics about Islam. We celebrated the

Muslim holiday of Ramadan, but not consistently or with any dedication. We were, however, consistently taught that Muslims don't do the "bad things" that Americans or Christians do. As if Muslims are sin-free?

Speaking of holidays, Christmas was a strange time for me as a child. I wanted gifts and a Christmas tree. I wanted to tell my friends what I got for Christmas, too. I wanted to fit in. At first, my parents would have a Christmas tree and some gifts for me, but that soon went away. Short of telling me that we were Muslim and didn't celebrate Christmas, they did not give me much more. There was no in-depth discussion on why Christmas should not be celebrated and no education on what made Islam different. .

So what was it like growing up in Middle America being an Arab family? It wasn't so bad. We were pretty normal, yet still very different in many ways. We ate different foods, spoke a different language at home, but for the most part, we were normal. Look, let's face it—America is a melting pot, so being different is actually normal. My siblings and I had lots of fun growing up and we were very close. I would say my parents did the best job they could, given their circumstances. Their situation could not have been easy. It would be like an English-speaking American moving his family to China with very little money, speaking little or no Chinese and having almost no help. It takes some courage, and for that, I applaud them and love them dearly.

Now as for my parents' involvement in our development as people, it was lacking in some areas. They loved us, but they really didn't raise us. We just grew up. Much like many families, they were probably just busy in survival mode. As a parent myself, I know how hard it can be. I cherish those years in Warren, Ohio. Most people who know me will tell you that I am not much of a softy, but I do get warm and fuzzy when I think about those days.

In most cases, I can hardly remember last week, but I can remember these years in so much detail. I can recall how I loved eating canned ravioli at the house of my best friend Tommy. We ate Arabic food all the time, so ravioli was a treat for me. I also remember how Tommy would sit and eat anything and everything that my mom would cook. He hated ravioli. I can recall the faces of the drivers whose cars we would bombard with snowballs from a hidden location in the woods. I remember each and every friend in detail. My wife finds it odd that I can remember stuff from thirty years ago, but I can't remember the name of someone I met ten minutes after they are gone.

Anyway, each of my siblings are now married with kids. Each one of them married in the traditional Muslim manner. The spouses were introduced by my parents, uncles, etc. My siblings had some input and the marriages were not completely forced. Regardless, I can't say that the marriages started in love, but that's just my view. That being said, each of their lives is their own story. I trust that the Lord has a plan for them as He has for me, and for you, for that matter.

Chapter 2
Moving On...God At Work!

I had just finished the sixth grade in 1983 when we moved to a suburb outside of Chicago. That only lasted a year and then we moved to San Diego. Yes, my family bought another convenience store. By this time, I was in the eighth grade. Life was good and pretty normal. I went to high school, chased girls and partied with my friends. Okay, I chased *lots* of girls and partied *a lot* with my friends. I graduated high school and began taking college courses. This is where my path in life changed.

It was in my second year of college when God really started working on me. I met the love of my life, Jessica, who just happened to be my best friend's cousin. I had been friends with Matt for about seven years. I had met his cousin Jessica once or twice during that time, but it was one specific night that I fell in love. Jessica and one of her friends were in San Diego visiting and Matt had arranged an evening out with Jessica and her friend. He was hoping to get to know Jessica's friend a little better. Okay fine, he was trying to pick her up. Anyway, Matt needed someone to keep Jessica company while he was courting her friend. That's where I came in. Matt figured it was a safe play; I was the last person Jessica would have interest in. Was he ever wrong!

I can remember the scene as if it just happened yesterday. Matt and I were waiting for the girls to arrive at his uncle's house. Matt was house sitting—two college guys, two college girls, a house and some spirits as I recall. It was the perfect storm. I was sitting on the couch when she walked in—long blonde hair, black tank top and khaki shorts. She was smoking hot and still is! I couldn't believe what I was seeing. This couldn't be the same cousin I had met as a child. Holy cow, I hit the jackpot!

My agreement to just keep Jessica "company" while Matt was courting was off the table—it was *love at first sight*! From that day on, Jessica and I were attached at the hip. As for Matt, he was less than thrilled with the idea of me dating his cousin. To be quite honest, it put a bit of a strain on our friendship. But look at us now, Matt and I started as friends, became family when I married Jessica and we are now brothers in Christ! Pretty cool how God works!

It wasn't any easy road for us. I can recall when it was all on the line. I had just been accepted to UCLA and our love was just beginning to take hold. I moved up to Los Angeles and Jessica stayed in San Diego, but we figured that we could make it work. Wow, those few months were bad and I couldn't take it anymore. The love of my life was slipping through my fingers. I had to do something. So I dropped out of UCLA and moved back to San Diego. My parents were beside themselves. How could I throw my life away for this "American girl"? What was I thinking?

My parents wanted an end to this relationship as soon as possible. They pleaded with me, but to no avail. My father made it clear, leave her or be cut off (no help with money, tuition, etc.). My father called and begged with members of her family to have her leave me. Some members of her family also agreed that she should consider a different path. Our love was steadfast. There were some challenging times, but we made it. Jessica has told me that she often considered if staying with me was best. Our backgrounds were so different, she was from a strong Christian family and I was from a Muslim family. Three kids later and with Christ as the center of our family, here we are. That is testimony to God's glory.

There is no question in my mind that Jessica was God's choice for me. I found Christ by getting on the right road. I did end up graduating from San Diego State University in 1994 with a BA in Journalism. I never went into any field remotely related to journalism, but here I am now, many years after college, writing a book. God knew I would need that education. He knows all!

It did not take long for my family to realize that Jessica wasn't going anywhere. I am sure that my family found it odd that this young woman would never hold a grudge or show any discontent for them. I am sure they found it even more odd that I didn't disown them, even though they were quick to cast me out. They soon accepted her and loved her dearly.

Chapter 3

Wedding Bells

M arriage was quickly becoming part of our future plan, but it seemed so difficult given our backgrounds. She wanted a traditional Christian wedding; I did not. At that time, I had no interest in Jesus and I just wanted a wedding, not a "Christian" wedding. Jessica gave in and we found a preacher (from the yellow pages) who agreed to marry us on my terms. It was okay for him talk about God, but not Jesus. I know this was hard for Jessica, but I also know that God had his hand in what was happening. God wanted this union.

Looking back now, I wish that I had known Christ at that time. I would have loved for Him to be the guest of honor instead of being asked to watch from afar. Regardless, Jesus was there at work—I just didn't know it. Jessica and I were married on July 25, 1998, after six years together. We got married at a beautiful golf course in San Diego. Jessica did not get the church wedding that she had dreamed about as a girl, but she got the guy that God wanted her to have.

The days leading up to our wedding were very stressful. I would have my mom, two sisters, my brother and some cousins attending—all Muslim. My father was not there. He decided to go overseas some months earlier. He was aware of the upcoming wedding, but chose to not be around. I have never held that against him; it's not my style to hold grudges. I'm sure he regrets the choice...or maybe not? Anyway, it was stressful because I wanted my wedding to be special, but I was so worried about offending my family. I just wanted everyone to feel comfortable.

The day before the wedding, we had the rehearsal and it was quite a show. My youngest sister went nuts! Apparently she felt hurt that I had not properly included them in the planning and I made my family feel like strangers. It was not intentional.

Nonetheless, those in attendance won't soon forget that day. It was the day before my wedding and my sister unleashed all of the family's frustrations on me right there in front of everyone. She called me things that you wouldn't call your worst enemy. Somehow, by God's grace, I just took it without retaliation and that is not one of my strong personality traits. I am a fighter! Although deeply hurt, I had to make quick amends or our wedding would be a disaster the next day.

The wedding went off smoothly. I never held a grudge against my sister and have always been there to help her and her family in times of need. She and I are very close to this day. In fact, she was the first family member that I shared my new faith with. On a side note: If you are considering getting married, don't do it outdoors in late July. I think our guests each lost two or three pounds from sweat. When Jessica and I celebrated our ten year anniversary, we had Pastor Jeremiah re-bless our marriage at Shadow Mountain Church in San Diego. Pastor Jeremiah played a huge role in my coming to faith in Jesus, as you will read more about in later chapters. This time Jesus was the guest of honor and it was all about Him! My family was not present, in fact, I did not invite them. I wanted this day to glorify Christ without any discontent.

Chapter 4
Life Was Changing Fast

Not long after we got married, Jessica was pregnant. We had our son "J" in 1999, and life was going great for us. I had been working in real estate for several years and I was doing very well, but something was missing. I found myself wanting something different. I was earning more than I could imagine being in my late twenties, but that wasn't enough. It was in the spring of 2000 when I notified my business partner, Jessica's uncle, that I was done and it was all his. I just walked away from a six-figure income with no plan.

Let me tell you it didn't take long for fear and panic to set in. What was I thinking? I had a family to support and had just quit my job. We only bought a home two months prior to this decision and now it was up for sale. Was I nuts? Not only did I think that I was nuts, but most everyone around me thought that I was nuts. I quickly began to sink into a depression and I could barely think straight. Sometimes Jessica and I would put "J" in his car seat and just drive for hours, going nowhere. I just wanted to be away from everyone. I thought for sure that I had ruined my family's life. Jessica, however, was solid as a rock.

It's amazing looking back now. She was caring for a new son and her idiot husband quit his high-paying career with no plan, yet she stayed strong. In fact, I don't remember a single time that she showed any fear, although I am sure she was terrified. She always had faith. On the other hand, I was in the fetal position quite often. Well I did finally come up with a plan.

My brother was my only support during that time, other than my wife. My parents could do nothing. They were living overseas at the time and had no idea what I was going through. My brother, a commercial pilot, was living in Texas. Jessica and I had spent six months with him and his wife while we were dating, so we had a good relationship (and still do). That was the plan—we would move to Texas. What was next. . .I wasn't sure.

I soon went off to Texas to buy a home for my family. It was a done deal. But what about work? I decided to follow in my brother's footsteps and become a pilot. Why not? It was the only plan on the table. We had plenty of money saved and it sounded like a good idea. To tell you the truth, I was just happy to have a plan.

Chapter 5

One September Day!

We sold our home in San Diego, packed up our family, and headed to Texas. I enrolled in a pilot training program. I recall meeting with the school and telling them I'd like to be ready to be hired by an airline in one year. They said it couldn't be done; it would take more time. I didn't care. I spent endless hours at the school, sometimes taking three to four flight lessons per day. Most of the students took one lesson per day and went home. The instructors at the school knew that I was on a mission and that if they had an open spot in their schedule, I was always ready to fly. That was the name of the game for instructors: build your hours up fast.

I quickly earned my private license, then my instrument license, and then my commercial license. I was now ready to get my instructor license. It was all happening so fast. It was almost one year exactly when I went for my instructor check ride with the FAA. I never studied so hard and so long for anything in my life. I was told that the FAA has a ninety-six percent first-time fail rate for instructors. That wasn't an option for me. I was on a mission.

That check ride took about six hours. I spent about five hours in an office with an FAA examiner who had nothing to do all day but keep his record of failing students strong. He asked me every question in the book, twice. I stood my ground. I was ready. Finally, he gave in and said that we could now go fly. We spent about an hour flying. He asked me to demonstrate some maneuvers and it was over. I passed!

As I look back now, I can hardly remember anything about that year that didn't have to do with flying. I was hardly ever home. I was either flying or working behind the counter of a small convenience store that my brother owned. I know what you're thinking, "What is the deal with Arabs and convenience stores?" I have no idea. Anyway, this store was in middle of nowhere. I mean this was a country store in the middle of Texas. I can recall sitting behind the counter from time to time pondering what happened to my life. Not long ago I had been a highly successful real estate agent in San Diego, California, and now I was ringing up beer sales to farmers in Azle, Texas. I have nothing against farmers or Texas. . .I am just saying it was a big change. Jessica, on the other hand, was solid. She seemed content just being home and raising "J". He was her rock. Mother and son filled each other's love tanks. I missed so much of his first two years. In fact, I missed it all. I was in my own world.

Finally, for the first time since I made the decision to change careers, I felt good. I was now instructing at the school. I was even instructing some students that started at the same time I did; most of them were still working on their instrument rating. Keep in mind I wasn't smarter than these guys, just more determined. Most of them were eighteen to twenty-two years old. I was now thirty with a wife and kid. No time to waste. I could now see the light at the end of tunnel. I just needed a few more months to build my flight time and I would be ready for the airlines. Everything seemed perfect. I had great connections through my brother at the airlines. I would soon be a commercial pilot.

One day changed everything. It was a normal morning and I went to school to instruct. I got my student briefed and off we went in our Cessna 172. It was a nice day to fly and we went to the training area to practice maneuvers. After about an hour of that we went to a local airport, about fifteen miles from our home airport in Arlington, to practice landings. We got permission from the tower to join the pattern. I think we were on our third approach and I asked the tower for another "touch and go". The controller responded in a firm voice, "You are clear to land". I corrected him saying we wanted to do a "touch and go", not land. He responded, "You are clear to land". I thought he had misunderstood my request, so I asked again. The response did not change, "You are instructed to land without delay!" I was terrified. I thought for sure I had done something wrong and that my career was over. My flying career was over, but not because of anything I had done.

I took the controls from the student and we landed at Spinks Airport. We were met at the plane by an airport official who asked us to gather our personal belongings, lock the plane and hand him the keys. *What in the world was going on?* We walked into the airport and made our way to the pilot lounge. Everyone was staring in silence at the TV. It was the morning of September 11, 2001. Like you and everyone in the world, I couldn't believe what I was seeing!

I called Jessica and told her I was on my way home. My brother wasn't reachable; he was in the air at the time. Of course, we feared that he was piloting one of those planes (not as a terrorist but as a crew member). I got home and stared at the TV in disbelief. I, like you, felt sad, scared and angry. But unlike you, I felt something different—guilt and shame. I couldn't believe that people of *my* heritage could do such an unspeakable act of hate. I wanted to peel my skin off and not be Arabic. I was so ashamed of "my people".

I knew these were radicals and don't represent the vast majority of the Arab world, but that logic wasn't relevant at the time. People were angry at the Arab world. Be honest, you probably had some hate and anger toward the entire Arab world as well. This was a horrible time for the world, for our country and especially for those who died and their loved ones. It was also a horrible time for each of us as individuals trying to deal with what took place. Many people lashed out at Arabs, as you know. Hate crimes jumped. It was scary to be an Arab. I was afraid for my family. I was feeling all the emotions that you felt; fear, sadness, confusion and anger. But I was also terribly ashamed. I think that's all I want to say about that.

On a good note, not everyone was filled with hate. I recall going to work at the beer store in Azle, scared to death. This was a farming town in rural Texas. Seriously, these guys drove up on tractors to buy diesel and beer. And there we were, Arabs in their town, right after September 11th. I expected the worst, but that's not what I got. Sure, there were some who just felt compelled to lash out with their tongues, but most people felt compelled to reach out a hand of compassion and love. Pretty awesome!

I also remember watching TV and seeing Christian women from various churches around the country escorting Muslim mothers and their children to and from school so they would not be harassed or hurt by those lashing out at Arabs. It brings tears to my eyes even as I write this today. *What kind of love is this?* These women were willing to put themselves in harm's way to protect the innocent, while in the streets of Palestine they were celebrating these horrific events that just took place? I found myself questioning everything that I ever thought about Islam. Was this the real Islam or just some radical view of Islam?

Were these terrorists doing what the Quran teaches? I didn't know. I know now. Unfortunately, Islam is not a peaceful religion. Fortunately though, most Muslims choose to be peaceful. It was also nice to see our nation come together and raising American flags, although I felt like an outsider. I know that more good will continue to come from this horrible event. For the thousands who lost their lives, there will be hundreds of thousands saved to Christ, maybe millions! September 11th was a major turning point in my life that led me closer to Christ.

As we all know, the world changed that day. Jessica and I knew that it was over; I wasn't going to be a pilot. Not only was the airline industry frozen, but the demand for Arab pilots was way down, to say the least. It goes without saying that our troubles were nothing in comparison to those who lost loved ones that horrible day. It was a dark time for all. By November of 2001 Jessica and I had packed up and moved back to San Diego. We drove the U-HAUL back on "J's" second birthday. As I recall, we celebrated his birthday at a barbeque place in Abilene, TX. It is the best barbeque west of the Mississippi (I think the place is called Joe Allen's). Did I mention that Jessica was also five months pregnant?

Okay, so what was I going to do for a career now? I had arranged with my former brokers a temporary job managing one of their real estate offices while I got my feet back on the ground. I am so grateful to them for that opportunity. Within six months of being back in San Diego, I was on my way to success again. Within a year, I was one of the top selling agents in the office and no longer the manager. Yes, once again, I was determined to succeed. Moreover, this time, I had something to prove to myself and those who thought I was an idiot to leave in first place.

Chapter 6

Blue-Haired Church Ladies

In March of 2002 we had our second child, another boy. Our life was back on track and things were good, but something was still missing. We had two kids and no sense of how to raise them. What are we? Muslim? Christian? Nothing? That was *not* okay. Jessica wanted direction from her husband. I didn't want to just raise them with no direction, but I had no direction myself. I decided it was time to seek the truth. Little did I know the truth had been seeking me all along.

Like so many people, I was trying to figure things out. I had always believed in God, but I was not going to believe in religion. I came up with so many of my own theories and I believed them! elieved that all religions were bogus; I believed that all "good people" would go to heaven. I believed Christians were brainwashed. It goes on and on. The funny thing is, I had never even opened a single book to study and justify any of my theories. It's funny how we can convince ourselves of anything. But something was now pulling at me, and I was ready to explore.

Being that my wife's family is Christian, I found myself at different churches from time to time. For the most part, I hated every minute of it. I felt out of place, afraid, confused and almost in panic at times. I felt judged. I could swear everyone was watching me. I can remember being at some of those services just knowing that everyone there knew that I wasn't one of them. I was afraid of the little blue-haired old ladies who greeted me at the door. I just knew they had an agenda to convert me.

I also met many of these "Christians". I can recall time after time when I would find myself in a conversation with a Christian and they would know nothing about their own faith. When I would put them on the spot with a tough question, they usually had no answer. Or worse, within minutes of a conversation, I could see them doubting and wavering, ready to just move on and avoid the confrontation. Look, I wasn't expecting them to know it all, but it would have been nice if they knew something. "Who wrote the Bible?", I would ask. Talk about a deer in headlights. You would think that if you are betting your life on this book, you might want to know who wrote it. The most common answer I got was, "Because the Bible says". Look, before you can quote a source, the source must be accepted as reliable.

I wasn't a believer. I had no reason to believe the Bible was factual and for anyone to use it as the answer to any question was meaningless to me. In fact, being raised in a Muslim family, I was told that the Bible was corrupt. Another common answer to questions was, "Well, I don't know the answer, but Jesus does love you". Who gives a hoot? I don't even know who this dude is. Oh, had someone just told me that He was God in human form.

Then there were the verse "quoters". Regardless of my question, they would just quote a verse from the Bible. What is that all about? How about the signs at football games? John 3:16. News-flash to my Christian brothers and sisters: those who don't know Christ just think you are nuts! They have no idea what your sign means! I had no idea. Of course, now I know what John 3:16 says: "For God so loved the world that he gave his only Son, that whoever believes in him shall not perish but have eternal life." But a sign with numbers is not preaching the Gospel.

Let's not leave out the door-knocking Christians. Come on man, going door to door, "selling" Christ. . .Really? Even to this day, I think this does more damage to the cause than service. To these Christians I say let God put you in front of the door that *He* wants you to walk through. Opportunities to serve the Lord are all around us; it doesn't have to be a sales job.

And let me tell you the thing I hated the most, the sledge-hammer Christians! It drove me nuts that these people believed that Jesus was the only way. Are you kidding me? I thought. How stupid! How arrogant! Yet, Jesus himself said, "I am the way, the truth, and the life. No one can come to the Father except through me" (John 14:6). Arrogant? Insane? Keep reading!

Chapter 7

A Sunday Morning Church Service

Sometime in the fall of 2002, Jessica had some family visiting from Washington State and they were Christians. They weren't just regular Christians; they are the type that makes no excuses for their faith. In fact, I used to think they were the real "nut jobs" of her family. I used to think that Stephanie (Jessica's cousin) and her husband Ron were as ignorant as could be. Little did I know it was me who was ignorant? Looking back now, Jessica's family was a great illustration of the Christian world. Some wore Christ on their sleeves and were a bit more "in your face," while others just walked with Christ, quietly, with love. For me, the quiet ones had the most impact! I don't mean any disrespect to Stephanie and Ron; 'ially admire them for their service to the Lord.

A Sunday Morning Church Service

Anyway, Stephanie and Ron wanted badly to go see this big time preacher, Pastor David Jeremiah. I was told that he was on the radio and on TV all over the world and his church was right there in San Diego. I went along to a Sunday service just to keep my wife happy. Yes, the church had the nice blue-haired old lady greeting people at the door, but something was very different this time. She was just a nice lady. Nobody was watching me and I didn't feel judged. The choir was magnificent and the worship music was piercing. Something was happening that day at Shadow Mountain Church.

Finally, about thirty minutes into it, he walked up on stage to preach. Here we go, I thought. Another white-haired preacher is going to spout off for forty-five minutes about this Jesus. He did preach about Jesus (as he always seems to do), but this time I was listening. I was interested. For the first time, I had actually heard this Gospel and it pierced my heart. Afterward, Jessica asked me how I liked the service, and I told her it was nice and suggested that we might come back sometime. She did not show it, but I know that she wanted to jump up and down.

Chapter 8

Meeting The Preacher Man

Soon after that service I started doing some reading on faith, God and religion. I was reading from a variety of secular books and a little from the Bible. As for the secular books, it's like a buffet of anything you want. I could find a book to tell me whatever I wanted to hear. Yet, every book said something different. I soon came to the conclusion that not every book could be right or true. It just wasn't logical. As for reading the Bible, the little that I read made no sense. I got to a point that I had a ton of questions, especially about Jesus.

It was March of 2003 when I decided to call this David Jeremiah dude and set up a meeting. I thought for sure I could break him and see through his line. Maybe I could even enlighten him a bit. First, I called the church and asked if I could meet the pastor, but they kindly tried to direct me to one of the associate pastors. How rude, I thought. I didn't like being blown off. Looking back now, I know that he has one of the busiest schedules of any pastor in America, so meeting one on one with everyone was just not possible. But I was determined. So I called his office directly. I told his secretary of my background and that I wanted to meet with him. Knowing Diane now, I'm sure she nearly fell out of her seat. Let's face it—it's not every day a Palestinian-born Muslim wants to chat with a Christian pastor about Jesus.

A few days later Diane called me back and said that Pastor Jeremiah would meet with me. I can only imagine what he was thinking. Was I for real? Was I going to kill him? This was post 9/11, after all. When I told Jessica that I was going to question this pastor, she said, "You can't just grill Dr. David Jeremiah." Why not? I asked her. This guy was the leader of this huge church and I wanted him to answer some tough questions.

I showed up that March 23, 2003 ready to go. I had a yellow pad full of questions. Not easy questions. I was ready to put this guy through the ringer. With grace and love, Pastor Jeremiah sat and answered my questions for nearly two hours. I recall his answers always went back to the Word of God. His own opinions never surfaced nor were they relevant. However, his love always surfaced. Let me tell you that Dr. David Jeremiah did not and does not have all the answers (which he freely admits) nor does any man.

Although he knew some basics about Islam, we hardly touched on that subject. It was all about Jesus. It was about an hour and a half into the meeting when he finally stopped me and changed my life. He said that if I was looking for a one hundred percent factual assurance that Jesus is who He said He is—the Son of God sent to pay the penalty for the world's sin and save those who believe—I wasn't going to find it with any research. He said that God would give me the assurance I need and the answers I needed if I first trusted in Him by faith. Faith is everything. Sure, it would be a "no brainer" to say ꞌ accept Jesus if He showed up at your door. When Jesus returns, there won't be any doubt as to who He is: "People will be terrified at what they see coming upon the earth, for the power in the heavens will be shaken. Then everyone will see the Son of Man coming on a cloud with power and great glory" (Luke 21:26-27).

God wants us to love Him as the humble lamb that died for us before we love Him as the almighty King, Pastor explained. Look at Thomas. . .even though the other disciples had told him that Jesus was raised from dead and that they had seen Him, he refused to believe: ". . .I won't believe unless I see the nail wounds in His hands, put my fingers into them, and place my hand into the wound in his side" (John 20:25). Jesus then appeared to Thomas and let him do just that. Then, Jesus told him, "You believe because you have seen me. Blessed are those who believe without seeing me" (John 20:29).

Pastor continued on and explained to me that I was infected with sin, just like everyone. He said that I would die of this infection if I didn't have the remedy. Jesus is the only remedy. He explained to me that I couldn't earn my way to heaven. God doesn't grade on a scale. You either arrive at heaven's gates still infected with sin, or cleansed by the blood of Jesus.

It was at that point that Pastor Jeremiah asked me if I was ready and willing to have faith. I was. He asked me if I was willing, right there in his office, to receive Christ. I did! Recently, Pastor Jeremiah shared with me that he was almost speechless that day when I said yes. I mean, it's not like Palestinians are accepting Christ on regular basis, but this one was ready. He prayed a simple prayer and I followed along out loud. It went something like this: God, I realize that I am a sinner and I fall short of your perfect holy standard. I ask that you forgive my sins and I want to receive your Son as my personal Savior. I want to live my life by your will and I need your Spirit to guide me daily. Amen. Can there be a simpler and a better thing to ask of God? No.

So why do so many resist? I think people want assurance without faith. Don't get me wrong, there is plenty of evidence, as you will see. But faith is still the key ingredient!

Chapter 9

"Born Again"...Now What?

So there I was, sitting in his office, a born again Christian...now what? Pastor Jeremiah said now I could seek the answers to my questions and God would provide the assurance I needed through the Word. He told me to go read the Bible! I told him that I had, but that it didn't make much sense. He asked me to go read the Gospel of John and call him back when I was done. I called him about week later to inform him that someone must have re-written my Bible, because it now made sense. It came to life.

And before we drift too far from the subject, what the heck is a "born again Christian"? I used to think these were the crazies at the airport. Wrong group! But seriously, what does the term really mean? It's quite simple. In speaking to a highly influential Jewish leader named Nicodemus, Jesus said, "Most assuredly, I say to you, unless one is born again, he cannot see the kingdom of God" (John 3:3). The discussion continued and Jesus went on explaining, "That which is born of the flesh is flesh, and that which is born of the Spirit is spirit" (John 3:6). We are all born once of the flesh; we all know how that works, but not all of us are "born again" of the Spirit. How does that work? Accepting Christ as your personal Lord and Savior is how that works.

So why is it that so many people who already go to church and have done so their whole lives and are Christians become "born again"? Aren't they already Christians? You don't get saved by going church and reading the Bible; you are not saved just because your parents have given their lives to Christ. It is a personal choice that each person has to make. It's a one-on-one talk with God, asking him to forgive your sins through the sacrifice of Jesus Christ. That makes you "born again" of the Spirit! Nothing else!

So anyway, I was now on a mission to find evidence. I believed faith, but I wanted to learn as much as I could. Let me tell you that the evidence is truly overwhelming that Jesus is who He said He is, the Son of God, God in the flesh. That's what this book is all about. Make no mistake about it, the evidence is overwhelming. In fact, once a person takes the time to do some homework, they'll see that it actually takes more faith to *not* believe. They will see that the Bible is an accurate historical record of real events, real people, and that it is God's Word.

Getting back on track and now born again, it was time for me to begin my personal relationship with God through Christ. To many, that statement makes no sense at all. Let me see if I can break that down. Now that I opened my heart and mind to God by accepting His Son by faith, I had the right to talk to God, to ask God questions, and He would hear me. I am not saying that God literally answered me by me hearing a voice, although God can do that if He chooses. He answered me by putting me in situations that would lead me to the answers I was seeking. He was doing that all along, but now I was aware of it. It's like God turned on a part of my brain and my heart that were not working before.

I was now aware of His doings. For example, I can't tell you how many times over the years I would be pondering some question about Christianity. I would just flip open the Bible and I would be exactly where I needed to be for the answers. Trust me, I am not that lucky. It was God. I can't tell you how many times I have walked into church to find that Pastor Jeremiah had written a sermon just to answer the very question that had been on my mind. Trust me, he isn't that good; he can't read minds (at least I hope he can't). These are works of the Lord. I talk to so many Christians who have the same experiences every day. Pastor Jeremiah has made the comment that new Christians are always saying how the Bible must have been re-written because they can now suddenly understand it. Interesting. . .isn't it?

Chapter 10

Tough Questions!

Now that I was a believer, I was really bent on getting some answers to the tough questions. I was thirsty and hungry for information. Unfortunately, I have learned that many new Christians just stop right here. They accept the Lord and everything is great. No! At this point, you are just an infant—just born. It is critical to continue to learn and grow. It is okay to have questions and doubts. It is normal. That is how we become mature Christians. It is a life-long process.

As discussed earlier, we are all infected with sin. We are not immediately sin-free when we accept Jesus. We are, however, immediately forgiven for all sin—past, present and future. We still live in the same sin infected body, but our spirit is fully healed. We can, however, treat our infection of the flesh with a large dose of Jesus daily. My point is that you must grow as a Christian. Two of the biggest questions for me were how and why Jesus was the only way. I began reading the New Testament. I wanted to understand what Jesus meant when He said: "I am the way, and the truth and the life; no one comes to the Father, but through Me" (John 14:6). "He who has seen Me has seen the Father" (John 14:9). "For unless you believe that I am He, you shall die in your sins" (John 8:24). These are such strong statements with profound implications!

Many Christians don't feel comfortable talking about this because of its implications. Let's cut to the chase: Jesus is claiming to be God in the flesh. This kind of exclusiveness just isn't politically correct. We want everything to be fair! God *is* fair. He is not exclusive. He will take anyone who will take Him. That's right, anyone. God will love and accept you if you will just accept Him first through Christ.

Why through Christ? Christ is the faith portion of this deal and the sacrifice. It is easy to say that you accept God when you see Him face to face. Who wouldn't? God wants us to accept His gift by faith. You see, that is how He knows we love Him as much as He loves us. God also wants us to see that we need His grace and forgiveness because we are all sinners (which we clearly are). Yet, some people think that they are "good enough". What is good enough? How can you be good enough if the standard is perfection?

Wait a minute. . .who said the standard is perfection? God said! God's standard has to be perfection, or He wouldn't be a God that we could honor. If He is perfect, then His standard must also be perfection, without flaw. So if God's standard is perfection and we can't be perfect, what are we to do? There is nothing that we can do except to let God do it all. God loves each of us so much that He was willing to come from heaven in the form of Jesus Christ with the purpose of dying for our sins (past, present and future). He would take our punishment if we would let him. Hold the phone—why should there be punishment to begin with? If God is so good and full of mercy, can't He just forgive us and move on? NO!

How could we honor God if He just let us get away with our sins? That would make God flawed. Think of it like this—if a judge let a confessed murder off scot-free, would that judge be honorable? I think not. What if that judge was the murderer's father and the judge agreed to take the gas chamber (or the cross) in place of his child? Wow! That would be an amazing father. That is what our Father God did for us when He became flesh in Jesus and died for our sin.

Can you love that much? How about all you dads and moms out there? Do you let your kids keep on doing wrong and forgive them every time without punishment? "Oh, Johnny, I forgive you for stealing again. Oh, Johnny, I forgive you, just please stop smoking pot." NO! We parents teach our kids right and wrong; we warn them once or twice (more for some of us) and then we impose the appropriate punishment. That is what Jesus did for us! But since the penalty for our sin is death, Jesus took that upon Himself. Why is death the punishment for even the smallest sin? Because God is without sin and God would be flawed if He accepted any sin. I am not going to honor anything flawed. Are you? But I will honor a God that would leave His holy place to become a man and allow himself to be punished mercilessly then crucified violently for me and for you. Can you love like that?

So what makes the crucifixion of Jesus enough for the whole world's sin? If you haven't gotten it yet, Jesus is God in the flesh. It took me a long time to get that point. In fact, my son "J" at age six made this so simple to understand. One day I asked him if he understood how Jesus could be God. He simply said, "Dad, Jesus is the body part of God". Hello, he was six! There are PhD's in theology that can't put it that clearly. So I guess that makes the Holy Spirit, the spirit part of God. The Father God, above us; Jesus, God with us; and the Holy Spirit, God in us. This is what is called the Trinity.

That's what makes His dying on the cross enough, Jesus and God are one. "Don't you know me, Philip, even after I have been among you such a long time? Anyone who has seen me has seen the Father." (John 14:9). Jesus replies to his disciple who wants to "see the father". So, you can see that because God and Jesus are one, God's sacrifice is more than enough.

Chapter 11

World Religions

Moving forward, I began looking into other religions and world views. I wanted to see how this all fit together. I wanted to be equipped to share and teach. Look, if Jesus is the only way, then all other religions must be false. Before going out and telling people that it's Jesus or nothing, I wanted to be educated. I'm still learning every day. I am not writing this book to bash anyone's beliefs. In fact, I know that people believe just as strongly in their way as I believe in Christ. However, just believing something with all your heart doesn't make it true.

People were certain when they believed that the world was flat. It isn't. There was a time when no one believed you could fly to the moon. We can. Given that my family is Muslim, my focus is Islam and the Judeo-Christian faith. These faiths are very intertwined as you will see. Nonetheless, let me briefly discuss what I have learned about some other beliefs first. Again, I am no expert and I encourage you to seek for yourself.

Atheists & Agnostics

By definition, atheists don't believe in any god. Or do they? In most cases, if you pin an atheist down and ask them some questions, you will soon find that they do believe in something, they just don't know what it is. There are basically two fundamental issues that can't be explained with this belief.

First is moral consequence. Ask an atheist why they live a moral life (assuming they do) if there is no God to answer to. Why not just rape, pillage and plunder? We could all be pirates. Of course, they will say that doing such things would have consequences that are not appealing (jail, for example). Okay, assuming there were no social consequences, would your average atheist choose to be a thief or murderer? I think not. Most atheists will soon admit that "something" guides their right and wrong choices. Something, huh?

Second, ask an atheist how life began. Now, this topic is deep. You could fill a football stadium full of books on how life began. That is not the purpose of this book. Generally speaking, however, there is no conclusive scientific evidence to show that life began without a creator. There is, however, powerful evidence *for* a creator. For example, if you just think about how complex our universe is, or think about how complex even a single strand of human DNA is, you can't say this was all by chance.

Intelligent design is from an intelligent designer. Don't take my word for this, do the research yourself. This topic is fascinating! Just ask an atheist how life began, or why we live by right and wrong and the foundation for their belief crumbles. What more can I say? A total lack of information can produce this kind of thinking.

What about agnostics? Generally speaking, they believe in some form of god or creator, but it stops there. I actually think that most agnostics just haven't taken the time to do some homework. They are quick to deny any belief that offends or doesn't satisfy everyone. Agnostics usually have very strong opinions, but very little substance to back the opinions. I think this sort of thinking is just lazy!

I guess you could say that I was somewhat of an agnostic even though I was Muslim by birth. Before doing any research, I was very vocal about my opinions. Agnostics usually dabble in many religions, accepting them all or the parts that they like. Other agnostics just flatly deny that any religion could be true. Either way, I have not heard a single argument from an agnostic that has a basis in fact or research. It is always about what they think or feel. Some agnostics are people pleasers who just want to acknowledge that all religions can be true because they don't want to offend anyone.

How can all religions be true? Hello, these religions don't say the same thing. Not even close! For my agnostic readers, Jesus Christ is not a religion! He is God in the flesh. It has nothing to do with being Catholic, Baptist, or Lutheran. Christianity is a simple "yes" or "no" deal. Do you believe that God became flesh in Jesus and died for your salvation? That is it! I don't really care what you call yourself.

On the other hand, how can all religion be false? Did God just put us here without any direction? We are here and He is in heaven. . .that's it? What kind of God is that? As you can see, this type of thinking doesn't sit well with me, because it has no basis in fact or common sense. I am a very logical thinker and these views are just not logical. Sure, it is very convenient and simple, but not logical or informed. To be honest, I would rather have someone tell me that they are an atheist than an agnostic. At least they are taking a position, wrong as it may be. Now that I have ticked off all of my agnostic and atheist readers, let's move on.

Eastern Religions

I mean no disrespect by bulking these together. I will confess that I have done the least amount of reading on religions such as Buddhism and Hinduism, but I have concluded the following from my research. Throughout history, there have been many "religions" and "spiritual guides" to come and go. These faiths teach so many different views that it would be impractical to cover them all. I don't deny that some of these teachings could possibly help improve one's life, but they don't teach anything that can grant one eternal life. I have no problem with living and seeking inner peace and harmony. As a Christian, however, I can have peace in God's Word. If I have God, I don't need anything else! In addition, these religions are manmade.

They all have a central figure that has, in some way or another, been able to get people to believe as he believes. Yes, Christianity has a central figure, but there is one big difference—Christ didn't just tell people what he thought to gain a following. Christ came and proved who He is. He performed miracle after miracle, including rising from the grave. Furthermore, the Bible is not one man's revelations or views; the Bible is a series of documents from various authors that have recorded real events. The Bible is very different!

Chapter 12

The Judeo-Christian Faith

As we get into this next section, I will cover Judaism and Christianity together. These two faiths are completely intertwined and dependent on one another. Together, they are the complete story of God. Judaism is Christianity unfinished. The Old Testament is the first half of the story and the New Testament is the rest. The Old Testament starts with, "In the beginning, God created the heavens and the earth" (Genesis 1:1). It goes on to tell in detail about how we all got here. It also explains in detail how this issue of sin came about and how God deals with it. Let me try to walk through this with you—but before I do, remember, nobody has all the answers to all the questions. If we did, faith would not be required.

So, God created man and then woman (Adam and Eve). They were humans just like you and me, having the ability to make free choices. They lived here on Earth in a perfect environment—the Garden of Eden. They walked and talked with God their creator. God loved them, as He loves you and me. God gave them one rule— not to eat from a specific tree in the Garden of Eden. When they disobeyed God and ate the fruit, they then knew for the first time what it was like to do wrong.

They were the first humans and they were infected with sin. Hold the phone; why did God put this tree there to begin with? Didn't God know that they would disobey? Of course He knew! God didn't want His creation (us) to love Him by default or by design; God wants us to love and trust Him by choice. That is why the tree was in the Garden of Eden. I like to think of that tree as the "Tree of Choice".

What meaning does love have if it is not given freely? You see, that is why the tree was in the Garden of Eden. God allowed choice so that we could freely choose or not choose to love and trust Him. From that point on, every human was infected with sin. This infection causes us to have the ability to choose right or wrong. But ultimately, this infection gives us the ability to choose or reject God.

The Old Testament is an amazing historical record of the Jewish people as well as an even more amazing prophetic writing. What do I mean? The Old Testament gave the Jewish people and the world a look at things to come. It gave the Jews a look into the future and foretold the coming of Jesus. Jews are, to this day, still waiting for the promised Messiah told about in the Old Testament. However, He has already come, they just don't believe. The problem is Jesus did not fit *their* idea of the King of kings. They were expecting Him to be the mighty ruler, not a poor carpenter from Nazareth.

Oh, how they loved to doubt. For example, even after knowing that Jesus had performed many miracles, the Jews still questioned. They had known of Him raising the dead, healing the blind, feeding thousands with just a few fish and healing the sick. Yet, the Pharisees and Sadducees often came to Jesus and asked Him to show them a sign. These were the elite religious leaders of the time. According to the Gospel of Matthew, Jesus would usually reply by just telling them to wait and see what happens next: "A wicked and adulterous generation looks for a miraculous sign, but none will be given it except the sign of Jonah" (Matthew 16:4). Jesus is referring to His own death and resurrection. In fact, it took seeing Jesus raised from the dead for one of His closest followers to believe!

Thomas was one of Jesus's disciples, and he said, "Unless I see the nail marks in his hands and put my finger where the nails were, and put my hand into his side, I will not believe" (John 20:25). This is a guy who walked with Jesus daily and saw these miracles first hand. But when Jesus rose from the dead and presented himself to the disciples, He granted Thomas's request: "Put your finger here; see my hands. Reach out your hand and put it into my side. Stop doubting and believe" (John 20:27). This is where we get the phrase "a doubting Thomas". For those of us who believe, we know that Jesus does rule the world and He is King. He is just not a King that the Jews can see in a palace in Israel today. But they will see Him again. When Jesus returns, He will be all that and more! But once again, God wants us to believe by faith before we see Him in all His glory.

Why did God need a New Testament in the first place? Did He make a mistake in the Old Testament? Of course not! God, in His wisdom, used the Old Testament to communicate several things to us. First, He explained to us how He created us and the universe in the book of Genesis. God then used the Old Testament to spell out right and wrong. He gave Moses the Law of the Ten Commandments. What's the purpose of the Law, you ask, if we can't keep it anyway? Great question! The purpose of the Law is to show us exactly that. God wants us to see through the Law that we are sinners, we are broken and we are not without fault! The Bible says it this way, "What shall we say, then? Is the law sin? Certainly not! Indeed I would not have known what sin was except through the law" (Romans 7:7).

After teaching us right and wrong, God used the Old Testament to teach us how He must deal with sin. Since God's standard is perfection, no sin can be acceptable and all sin is equally offensive to God. Hold the phone—are you saying that murder is just as bad as lying? Yes! Look, if we believe that God is all good and all perfect, than He can't possibly be okay with any sin. If God can tolerate sin at any degree, then He is not perfectly good. Since God cannot tolerate any sin, then the penalty for any sin is death! But that's not fair, you say. But it is perfect! So, God proceeds to use the Old Testament to show us how He deals with this sin.

God sets up the sacrifice system. Jews would bring God their best animal as a sacrifice for their sin. Make no mistake; God wanted it to be clear that only a perfect sacrifice can cover sin. God was showing us that we cannot cover our sin through our own efforts. We cannot just do "enough" good works. We have to allow Him to forgive our sin.

Today, Jews practice forgiveness through prayer and repentance as they wait for the Messiah, but He has already come. Jesus will return again, however. But on His return, it will be too late to believe. As you can see, God used the Old Testament to show us what was yet to come—Jesus, the final sacrifice.

I don't mean to go off subject, but stay with me. One question I used to have was, why did God choose the Jewish people to bring us all this? For many Arabs, this is a big deal. Jews are the enemy. Here is the answer: I don't know and it really doesn't matter! I am just glad that God loved us all enough to send us the Message. Jesus came for everyone, not just Jews. In fact, look at His final instruction to the disciples before ascending to heaven: "All authority in heaven and on earth has been given to me. Therefore go and make disciples of all the nations. . ." (Matthew 28:18). He did not say to go make disciples of just the Jews, but *all* the nations.

Come to think of it, the Jews haven't had it very easy being God's "chosen people". Look at all that they have gone through (and still go through) as a people. That's right, I feel sorry for the Jewish people. In fact, I now love the Jewish people. My God and Savior came to show His love through these people, so how can I not love them? Jesus himself was Jewish. Unfortunately, I hated them not too long ago. What? It's almost shameful to admit, but true nonetheless.

Even though I was raised in America and my family was not radically Muslim in any way, we were still against Jews. That's just the way it is with most Arab families. Being uninformed about history, most Arabs simply believe that the Jews have stolen their land. Don't be fooled to think that most Arabs don't feel this way. That's just hogwash! Don't think that most Arabs want to live in peace, side by side with Jews. It's just not the case.

I am not a historian, but I do know that the Jewish people first conquered Canaan (modern day Israel) nearly two thousand years before Muhammad was even born. Islam wasn't even a religion and the land was occupied by godless, immoral pagans—not by Muslims. Okay, so if Arabs really want Jews gone, how can there ever be peace in that region? There is only one way: Christ! Yes, loving and following Jesus will turn any Jew hater to a Jew lover overnight. I would bet the same applies to many Jews; they don't really want peace. They want the Arabs out of Israel. Jews need Jesus just as badly as the Arabs need Him.

Getting back on track, let's take a deeper look at some of the prophecy in the Old Testament that points to Jesus. Scholars show us that there are sixty major messianic prophecies and approximately two hundred and seventy ramifications that were fulfilled in one person, Jesus Christ. Using the science of probability, researchers have found the chances of just forty-eight of these prophecies being fulfilled in any one person to be only one in ten to the one hundred fifty-seventh power. I am not a math genius, but that is a huge number. By the way, all of these prophecies were known to have been made some four hundred years or more before Christ appeared.

In addition, Jesus had no way of purposely fulfilling most of these prophecies. For those of you who might think that Jesus was a fraud, here are just some of these prophecies: "But you, Bethlehem Ephrathah, though you are small among the clans of Judah, out of you will come for me one who will be ruler over Israel, whose origins are from of old, from ancient times" (Micah 5:2). This was written some seven hundred years before Jesus was born in Bethlehem. But

Jesus was never the ruler over Israel? The story is not over. . .Jesus will rule when he returns.

Here is another prophecy that was fulfilled and Jesus had no control over. "The days are coming, declares the Lord, when I will raise up to David a righteous Branch, a King who will reign wisely and do what is just and right in the land. In his days Judah will be saved and Israel will live in safety. [The Jewish nation was once in two parts, Israel to the north and Judah to the south.] This is the name by which he will be called: The Lord Our Righteousness" (Jeremiah 23:5-6). We know that Jesus's family line goes back to David. Jesus is who this prophecy is referring to. "Therefore, the Lord himself will give you a sign: The virgin will be with child and will give birth to a son, and will call him Immanuel" (Isaiah 7:14). *Immanuel* is not just a name, but an adjective meaning savior. Isaiah is saying here that He will be known as the Savior. As of today, there has only been one born of a virgin—Jesus Christ, Savior. Another prophecy fulfilled.

On a side note, even the Quran testifies that Jesus was born to the Virgin Mary in Sura 3:47: "O my Rabb! How can I have a son when no man has ever touched me?" Here is another Old Testament prophecy: ". . .See, your king comes to you, righteous and having salvation, gentle and riding on a donkey, on a colt, the foal of a donkey" (Zechariah 9:9). This event took place some five hundred and fifty years later when Jesus rode into Jerusalem one week before being crucified. Yes, he rode in on a colt.

Jesus's betrayal by Judas was also foretold in Psalm 41:9: "Even my close friend, whom I trusted, he who shared my bread, has lifted up his heel against me". I could go on and on with Old Testament prophecy that points right to Jesus, but I think you get the point. Furthermore, you can see that most of the prophecy was out of Jesus's control, for those who think He rigged it. And for those who think that His followers put these prophecies in the scripture after the fact, not so. There are existing Old Testament manuscripts that predate Jesus and His followers by hundreds of years.

Can you can see how Judaism is part one of the Jesus story? Given the history of the Jewish people and the unprecedented persecution they have gone through, I can see how they might be looking for a king to stop their pain and bring them to glory. However, I just pray that the Jewish people could look beyond their earthly needs and really look to their heavenly needs. If they did that, they would see that Jesus is the Messiah that was promised. He will bring them to glory. He rules with a righteous hand.

Once again, we come back to the same theme—Jesus wants us to accept him by faith. It won't mean a thing to Jesus if you only believe when you see Him face to face. Remember what Jesus said to his disciple Thomas: "Because you have seen me, you have believed: blessed are those who have not seen and yet have believed" (John 20:29).

Chapter 13

But Is The Bible Reliable?

Okay, so the Old Testament is filled with prophecy about Jesus, but what if the Bible isn't even reliable? What if it is corrupt? Great questions! In fact, these are *critical* questions. Let's face it, if the Bible we have today isn't reliable and isn't God's message to us, then who cares what it says! However, if we can prove beyond a reasonable doubt that the Bible is reliable and true, then anything that contradicts it must be false. Yes, I said it; anything that contradicts the Bible must be *false* simply by definition. I know this isn't what people like to hear in today's times. It offends many and it might offend you. It used to offend me. But put your emotions aside for a second and think about it logically.

For example, ocean water can't be salty and salt-free at the same time. Gravity either exists on our planet, or it doesn't. A woman is either pregnant or not. It can't be both ways. Either God came to earth in the form of Jesus Christ, died and rose again, or He did not. It's that simple. Since none of us were there, the evidence will still need to be accompanied by faith. But God, in all His wisdom, knows just how little faith we actually have, so He made sure that the evidence would be overwhelming. We just have to want to look into the facts. We have to want to seek truth.

"Okay, show me that the Bible is true," you say. Fine, but if your heart is not open and you are just reading for the sake of reading, stop and close the book. It won't do any good. But if you are willing to open your mind and open your heart and ask God to show you the truth, then keep reading.

Let's start by looking at some facts about the Bible. Today's Judeo-Christian Bible consists of the thirty-nine books of the Old Testament and the twenty-seven books of the New Testament. There are more than forty known authors from every walk of life, including kings, poets, peasants, fishermen, doctors, scholars and statesmen. The Bible was written over forty generations covering more than one thousand five hundred years. It was written on three different continents: Asia, Africa and Europe. It was written in different places such as jail cells, dungeons, deserts and the wilderness. It was written in three different languages: Hebrew, Aramaic and Greek.

The Bible has been read by more people and published in more languages than any other book in history. So what? Here is the kicker: given all this, these books do not contradict each other. They all tell the same consistent story. That is some powerful evidence in itself. I would be more skeptical if the Bible had one author or was just "revealed" to one man in his visions, like the Quran for example. No, the Bible is not one man's vision; it is a historical record of actual events.

How did we end up with sixty-six books? Why not more? Why not less? Great questions! As for the thirty-nine books of the Old Testament, these are the same thirty-nine books that Jewish leaders agreed upon sometime shortly after the Temple in Jerusalem was destroyed around AD 70. There is not much, if any, controversy with the Old Testament. The Jews were known for being great recorders and protectors of their faith. Many archeological finds have confirmed their authenticity. As for the twenty-seven books of the New Testament. . .there is some controversy (or it seems that way).

Yes, there are several known writings that do not appear in today's Bible. Sometime around AD 397, Christian church leaders gathered at a council meeting to debate this very topic. The council used three main questions to determine what writings were authentic:

1. Were they written by apostles or their close associates (who all personally saw Jesus)?
2. Were the writings widely recognized by local churches as messages from God?
3. Were the writings in line with traditional Christian teachings?

It used to really bother me that this "council" got to pick and choose what they wanted to include until I understood it better. Let me put it this way: what if I wanted to have this book included in the Bible? It is in line with Christian teachings? I believe it is God inspired. Does it belong in the Bible? No. There has to be criteria.

Now that we have some facts about the Bible, let's look to see how reliable it really is. Well, let me start with this—can you think of any other book or writing that has been scrutinized more than the Bible? Let's face it, there has never been a time in history that some group was not out trying to disprove or discredit the Bible. It has been burned, banned and outlawed. And yet, at no point has it been refuted with credible evidence. In fact, many of those who have tried to disprove it become believers themselves.

Chapter 14

More On How The Bible Came To Be

Let's take a look at how we got the actual written versions of the New Testament. Initially, the stories about Jesus were passed on by word of mouth. Keep in mind, the believers of that day expected that Jesus would be returning in their lifetime, and recording these events wasn't on their minds at first. Jesus, however, never promised to return in their lifetime at all.

It was not until around forty or fifty years after Jesus ascended to heaven that the first writings appeared. These writings were then copied by hand into manuscripts and distributed. There are today more than five thousand three hundred known Greek manuscripts. Within these manuscripts, there are known to be different writing styles, word choices and other minor variations, as would be expected. Nonetheless, the message in these manuscripts is consistent. I would personally be more skeptical if they were all identical. There is no other known historical writing that even comes close in number of manuscripts. Homer's *Iliad* comes in second to the New Testament with six hundred forty-three and it is deemed accurate and taught in schools. Interesting?

How about archeology? As we have said before, there has never been a book to receive more scrutiny from critics than the Bible, yet archeology has not turned up any evidence that discredits the Bible. In fact, there are numerous findings that prove and strengthen the reliability of the Bible. For example, the Dead Sea Scrolls. The Dead Sea Scrolls consist of roughly one thousand documents including texts from the Jewish Bible. Discovered between 1947 and 1965 in caves, in and around the northwest shore of the Dead Sea in the West Bank, the texts are of great religious and historical significance as they include practically the only known surviving original copies of Biblical documents made before 100 AD. Here are some of the books found: thirty-nine from Psalms, thirty-three from Deuteronomy, twenty-four from Genesis, twenty-two from Isaiah, eighteen from Exodus and many more.

Most importantly, scholars have concluded that these historical documents are in line and consistent with the Bible we have today. This finding tells us that the more recent manuscripts were, in fact, copied accurately. To date there have been no significant findings that discredit the Bible. And don't forget, many of the people examining the findings are not pro-Bible. In fact, they would love nothing more than to disprove it.

Chapter 15

Early Opposition Against Jesus

How about those who wanted to stop this Jesus stuff in the first place? The first groups who wanted to discredit Jesus were the Jews and the Romans who put Him to death to begin with. After finding out that Jesus's body was not in the tomb, these two groups had everything to gain by coming up with His corpse. They could have put an end to this whole uprising. They did not find His body. Well, maybe His disciples stole the body, you say. And maybe they just wanted to start a cult of believers. I guess that could happen?

There is one problem with that theory though: if these disciples knew that the whole thing was a hoax, why would they allow themselves to be killed for their faith? That's right, they were all persecuted and given the choice to denounce Jesus or die. They chose death. Some were crucified, some stoned to death and others beheaded. Would you die for something that you knew was a lie? I think not. In fact, these very same disciples didn't even begin preaching until after they saw Jesus back from the dead.

We read that while Jesus was being tried, beaten, and crucified, they hid and denied even knowing Him. While Jesus was being arrested, a woman in the mob crowd saw Peter and pointed him out to the authorities as being one of Jesus's followers. Peter responded with: "Woman, I do not know him" (Luke 22:57). But immediately after seeing Jesus face to face, raised from dead, Peter and the others hid no longer. They now publicly proclaimed Jesus, Lord and Savior.

Chapter 16

Faith Is The Only Way

I could go on and on for pages writing about evidence, science, history and archeology, but that is not the purpose of this book. The purpose of this book is not to show you Christ by *proof*, but to show you Christ by *faith* and back it up with proof. That is the only way! Let me put it this way: there are many people much smarter than I, who know much more about the proof, yet they do not believe. How can it be that two different people can look at the same evidence and one believes, while the other does not? Faith is the only way! God wants you to trust Him by faith. He wants you to surrender to Him, not surrender to the proof. He wants you to give your heart to Him, not to the proof. He wants you to have a loving relationship with Him, not the proof.

If you really want to take this a step further, faith is required in any religion. Let's look at Islam for example, which we will be discussing in the next chapters. No Muslim can show me Muhammad any more than I can show him Jesus. So, Muslims believe by faith. The same goes for Buddhists, Mormons and even atheists. So, the real question is, what are you putting your faith in?

Chapter 17

Islam & Christianity...
Let's Compare!

I want to now take a side by side look at what Islam offers compared to Christianity. Although the "evidence" overwhelmingly proves the Bible's accuracy, let's put that aside and just look at what the two faiths say about life, salvation and eternity. Let's look at the Bible and the Quran and take them at face value. Then, I challenge my Muslim readers to decide by faith who they should follow—Muhammad or Jesus.

It's important to state that as we look at Islam and compare it with Christianity, this is a comparison of two faiths, (two books) *not* a comparison of the people who follow these faiths. Why is this important to mention? Well, because there are people on both sides who do not represent what the faiths really teach. I know plenty of "Christians" who talk the talk, but don't walk the walk. Also, it must be said that not all Americans or westerners are Christians. Most Muslims have a false belief that all Americans are Christians and when they see "American culture" played out on TV, they think all Christians act like this. Not the case.

The same can be said regarding Christians. Many Christians think that all Arabs are Muslim. Not the case. In fact, most Muslims around the world are not Arabs. Many Christians believe that most Muslims are terrorists or radicals—far from the truth. As you can see, it is critical that we only compare doctrines, not people. In addition, it is not my desire to get into the debate about terrorism and Islam. I am not here to debate Jihad or women's rights; politics is not on my agenda either. I simply want to examine these books to see which one is God's Word. They cannot both be!

Let's take a look at some basic facts about Islam and the Quran. There are approximately 1.4 billion Muslims in the world today. Islam's prophet is Muhammad. He was born in AD 571 in Mecca. The Quran was reputedly revealed in Arabic, to Muhammad, by

Allah through the angel Gabriel over a period of twenty-two years (610-632 AD). As these revelations were revealed, Muhammad would memorize and recite them to his followers who would also memorize them. Memorizing large amounts of information was not out of the ordinary during those times.

The Quran consists of one hundred and fourteen chapters called "Suras". The Suras are not in any real chronological order. For the most part, they are arranged from longest to shortest. However, it is believed that the longer revelations came later in Muhammad's life. The written Quran that exists today was compiled some twenty years after Muhammad died in 632 AD, at the age of sixty-two. The third *caliph* (political leader), Uthman, was responsible for gathering all written text along with the memorized revelations in order to compile an official Quran. Once completed, he ordered any other text to be burned.

The basic beliefs of Islam are that there is only one god (Allah) and that Muhammad was the last of many prophets that came before. As for salvation, for the most part, those who believe in Allah and his prophet Muhammad and do good works will be saved. Yet, there is no clear definition of "good works" and how much needs to be done. In addition, Allah can save whomever he wishes. There is a major focus in Islam on Allah being so merciful that he can choose to spare anyone he chooses. This poses a big issue. This would imply that Allah might choose to save the worst of sinners and destroy the holiest. If that is the case, then Allah is not just. If Allah is not just, then his display of mercy is really a display of power. As you can see, salvation in Islam is very uncertain; only one who dies during Jihad as a martyr has assurance of "paradise".

As Christians, our salvation is one hundred percent assured in Christ. In believing that God loved me enough to come down from Heaven and pay the penalty for my sin, I am forgiven and I will be with Him for eternity. I am not required to fulfill any duties. In fact, I can't do anything that surpasses what He has done for me. As a forgiven, saved Christian, I live morally and change my ways to honor God. I do good deeds out of gratitude, not obligation. Look at it like this: do you want your kids to obey you because they are scared and have to, or do you want them to obey you out of love?

This salvation plan in Christianity displays real mercy, because it is just. It is offered to everyone.

God created us each with free will, with the purpose that we would be able to accept his salvation by choice. You see, it's all about free will. Without free will, there is no love between us and God. In fact, without free will, there is no love between us and anyone. Free will is a main component of love.

What about people who have never heard about Jesus or those who lived before Jesus? How can they choose and accept this just salvation? This is a great question. Here is the simplest answer that I can give you. If God is love and God is just, then how about we just leave that up to Him and believe that He has that worked out? How about we just worry about our relationship with Him and trust God to deal with each of His other creations as He sees fit. We don't know how He will deal with them, but we must believe that He will deal with them in love and that they will have the option to accept His love. We shouldn't need God to explain how He will do that. He is God.

As we move forward, please keep in mind that the god of the Quran (Allah) and the God of the Bible are not the same, as Muslims believe. The God of the Bible showed Himself in the flesh as Jesus Christ. The Quran disputes this critical point. In fact, Allah was one of three hundred and sixty idol gods that were worshiped in Mecca when Muhammad began his ministry. Muhammad identified this "moon god" (Allah) to be the one true god. It is true that both Muslims and Christians believe that there is only one God, but when you ask each to identify their god's characteristics, it becomes very clear that these are two *very* different gods.

Islam has five foundational practices or duties that every Muslim must observe. They are knows as the Five Pillars (some say there are six):

1. **The Creed** *(Kalima):* "There is no god but Allah, and Muhammad is the Prophet of Allah." This is the core of Islam. One must state this aloud publicly in order to become a Muslim. The creed is said over every new born, making them "Muslim by Birth."

2. **Prayer** *(Salat):* Muslims are required to pray five times per day (upon rising, at noon, at mid-afternoon, after sunset and before retiring for bed). Prayer in Islam is very mechanical with specific procedures—standing, kneeling, hands on face and so on. Prayer is to be done while facing east toward the Mecca and the Kaaba. The prayers themselves are prescribed selections to be recited from the Quran. The prayers must be recited in Arabic, so non-Arab speaking Muslims must learn Arabic. Allah only understands Arabic? In Christianity, prayer can be done anytime and is a one-on-one loving communication between a believer and his or her Father in heaven.

3. **Charity** *(Zakat):* Muslims are required to give two and a half percent of their income for the destitute. Christians are to give ten percent (or at least they should). Although Christian giving is clearly defined in the Bible, our salvation does not depend on this or any other duty. Christians give to honor and obey God.

4. **Fasting** *(Ramadan):* During this holy month, Muslims do not eat or drink from sunrise to sunset. This fasting develops self-control and promotes devotion to Allah. Fasting is also a part of Christian life and serves similar purposes, but is not a specific requirement.

5. **The Pilgrimage** *(Hajj):* Each Muslim is required to make the trip to Mecca and perform certain rituals at the Kaaba. There are some exceptions regarding making this trip such as physical restrictions for some Muslims.

6. **Holy War** *(Jihad):* This is a religious duty associated with the Five Pillars. This duty requires men to go to war (when the situation warrants) to defend and spread Islam. If one dies while performing this duty, he or she is assured entrance to paradise. As we all know, Jihad is a major world issue. Terrorisim stems from this.

Chapter 18

What Does The Quran Say About Jesus?

Let's now take a closer look at what the Quran has to say compared to the Bible. As you will see, there are some similarities, but there are also many significant differences between the Quran and the Bible. The most important differences are regarding who Jesus Christ is. These differences stem from the core belief Muslims have, that our Bible is corrupt and has been altered. This fundamental error in thinking is what stops most Muslims from the truth.

Jesus is a major figure in Islam. That's right! Jesus is mentioned some ninety-three times in the Quran—more than any other figure in the Quran. How can any Muslim ignore the fact that their version of Jesus is very different than the Bible's? Why not investigate this?

I mean, if the Quran was really given to Muhammad from Allah through the angel Gabriel, then it can't be disproven. Why is it *haram* or sinful to question Islam? I would think that Muhammad would encourage it if his message is divine. The Bible instructs Christians to question and seek answers, not just follow blindly. In 1 John 4:1 we read, "Dear friends, do not believe every spirit, but test the spirits to see whether they are from God, because many false prophets have gone out into the world."

Islam wants you to believe that God revealed his entire message to one man. Since there were no witnesses to these visits from the Angel Gabriel, a Muslim must believe Muhammad through blind faith. Back to Jesus. . .isn't it interesting how when it comes to discussing any religion, we always end up debating the same issue—who is Jesus? So what does the Quran itself really say about Jesus and the Bible? Before we dive in, please know that my Muslim friends will say that any non-Arabic translation of the Quran is not reliable. I am not sure how to respond to this, but to just say, are you serious? I think the world is advanced enough now to translate the Arabic language.

Nonetheless, if my Muslims friends want to challenge this, then they should get their Arabic Quran out and compare for themselves. Plus, are we to really believe that the Creator of the Universe insists on communicating with us only in Arabic...seriously?

Okay, let's move on. The Quran does say that Jesus was born of a virgin:

> When the angels said, "O Maryam! Allah gives you the good news with a Word from Him that you will be given a son: his name will be Messiah, Isa *(Jesus Christ)* the son of Maryam. He will be noble in this world and the Hereafter; and he will be from those who are very close to Allah." (Sura 3:45).

> Hearing this, Maryam said, "O my Rabb! How can I have a son when no man has ever touched me?" (Sura 3:47).

> He said: "Don't be afraid, I am merely a messenger from your Rabb to tell you about the gift of a holy son." She said:

"How shall I bear a son, no man has ever touched me nor am I unchaste?" (Sura 19:19-20).

The Quran says that Jesus performed miracles:

Then Allah will ask: "O Isa *(Jesus)* son of Maryam *(Mary)*! Recall my favor upon you and to your mother, how I strengthened you with the Holy Spirit, so you could speak to the people in cradle and in old age, how I taught you the Book, Wisdom, the Taurat *(Torah)* and the Injeel *(Gospel)*. How you were able to make the figure of a bird out of clay, by My permission, how you breathed into it and changed it into a real bird, by My permission. How you can heal the born blind and the lepers by my permission. How you could bring the dead body back to life by my permission" (Sura 5:110).

The Quran says that Jesus was righteous and supported by the Holy Spirit:

> We have exalted some above others. To some Allah spoke directly; others He raised high in ranks; to Isa *(Jesus)* the son of Maryam *(Mary)* We gave clear Signs and supported him with the Holy Spirit (Sura 2:253).

As you can see, there are some parts of Islam and Christianity that are similar. However, there are some major differences.

There are major differences that go directly to the core of why so many Muslims won't consider Christianity. These issues are critical and have to be dealt with. These objections need a response! Here are some.

Muslim Objection:

The Quran teaches that Jesus was created by Allah and is not God in the flesh.

The Christian Response:

The real issue is that most Muslims think that Christians believe that a "man" is our God. Unfortunately, this misunderstanding is our own fault as Christians. How often do you see a sign that says Jesus is God? Well, to a Muslim, that reads "a man *is* God". These signs should read God is Jesus. You see, God, in all His power, chose to become a "man". Jesus (the man) did not choose to become God. God can do that. . .He is God! Christians do claim that God and Jesus are one, but do not claim that a "man" is God.

There is a big difference. Jesus and God are one? Try not to over think this. If God chose to become a "man," then God and that "man" are *one*. God, like so many other things, is more than just one part. For example, when you open a window to let some sun in, does the actual sun come down from the heavens into your living room? I hope not. Sunlight does come in, however. Even with the sun still in the heavens, you feel the sun on your skin. The sun is more than just the sun.

How about me, Sam? I reveal myself to my kids as a father. I reveal myself to my wife as a husband. I am a father, husband and a friend—all still Sam. God reveals himself as God the Father who created all things; God the Son, the human version sent down to be the role model and sacrifice; and God the Spirit, living in each of us, directing our thoughts and feelings. Guess what...we just covered the response to the next objection that Muslims have—the Trinity.

Muslim Objection:

The Quran says that God does not consist of three parts as the Bible teaches:

> So believe in Allah and His Rasools and do not say: "Trinity". Stop saying that, it is better for you. Allah is only One Deity. He is far above from the need of having a son! (Sura 4:171)

The Christian Response:

Go back and read the last response above. In addition, not only does the Quran say that there is no "Trinity," but it defines it as God, Jesus and Mary...not Father, Son and Holy Spirit as the

Bible actually teaches. This does not exist anywhere in the Bible. Christians do not, in any way, claim that Mary is one with God or divine in any way. This, again, is Muhammad's misunderstanding of the Christian faith.

If he had read the scriptures, he would not have made this claim since it does not appear. I realize that my Muslim friends will now say, "But the Bible was corrupt." We will get to that issue soon enough.

Muslim Objection:

The Quran says that Jesus was not the son of God and seems to even imply that Allah "begot" a son like I "begot" my sons. Again this shows how Muhammad clearly misunderstood this idea of God showing Himself in human form. Jesus is God in human flesh. That's very different than the notion that God "begot" a son:

> Never has Allah begotten a son, nor is there any god besides him (Sura 23:91).

It is not befitting to the majesty of Allah that He Himself should beget a son (Sura 19:35).

The Christian Response:

Once again, we have a complete misunderstanding. Muhammad is saying that Christians must believe that God somehow had a son like you or I would have a son and that this would be beneath God's standards. Muhammad seems to be saying that Christians believe God had some sort of "relations" with Mary and begot a son. Otherwise, why would Muhammad label anyone who says God had a son as an "infidel"? Muhammad makes it clear how wrong this would be. Muhammad's argument is that Jesus, like Adam, was born from miraculous circumstances and that Christians should stop saying that Jesus was begotten like you and me. Christians agree and that is not what we are saying about Jesus! Muhammad just did not understand it, like many other things. By the way, saying that Christians believed this was a good way for Muhammad to get new followers to turn away from Judeo-Christian ways. Muslims today still use this same wrong logic.

Let me say this as clearly as possible. Christians do not believe this and never have. The Bible does not say or even remotely imply that God had "relations" with Mary. When Christians say Jesus is the Son of God, we don't mean it literally. We are saying that Jesus is the human revelation of God. Jesus is very unique in every way. Calling Him the Son of God is just a way of saying that Jesus is intertwined with God, one with God.

How about this—Jesus refers to Himself in the Bible as the "Son of Man". Should we take that literally? No. Jesus is simply saying that He is intertwined with mankind like no other. "Son of _____" is a figure of speech, nothing else. Here in America, we use the term "Son of the South." Are we implying that this person's father had relations with the "South" and they had a child together? Hello? No, we are saying that this person is southern down to the core: the clothes they wear, the food they eat, how they talk, etc.

This term is also used in the Middle East. *Ibn el-Nil* (Son of the Nile) is the name of a very famous Egyptian drama film from the 1950s. Do you think the main character's father had relations with the Nile River to have him? Of course not! The term "Son of the Nile" implies that this character was deeply rooted in ways of the Nile River region and its people.

Muslim Objection:

The Quran says that Jesus was not crucified:

...Whereas in fact, neither did they kill him nor did they crucify him but they thought they did because the matter was made dubious for them (Sura 4:157).

The Christian Response:

Okay let's start with this: if you just look at the evidence presented earlier regarding how unlikely, if not impossible, it was for the Bible to have been altered. Remember, we have manuscripts from all over the world, in different languages, in different time periods of history that say the same thing. How could they all be corrupt? Maybe the disciples changed it from the beginning then all the manuscripts would say the same corrupt thing, the skeptic might say. Not so fast. If these disciples knew that Jesus was not crucified and that the whole thing was a fraud, would they have been willing to die for this lie? That is exactly what happened, as you read earlier.

Maybe the disciples weren't really killed? Come on, let's not let skepticism turn to stupidity. This would mean that Christianity was the biggest hoax in the history of the world; this would mean that Jesus and the disciples were nothing but a bunch of cheats and liars. Yeah, sure, this goes right along with what they decided to allow in the Bible: "Love one another". How can the Bible be about love and forgiveness if it was written by a bunch of liars? I think it would have been more about sex, war and power. Like the Quran perhaps?

We can clearly see that the Bible and the Quran do, in fact, conflict. Not only that, but they conflict on the most critical question—who is Jesus? The Quran claims that Jesus was a righteous and noble prophet. Jesus himself claims to be the Son of God, God in human form and the only path to God: "I and the Father are one" (John 10:30).

"No one can come to me unless the Father who sent me draws him, and I will raise him up at the last day" (John 6:44). "Moreover, the Father judges no one, but has entrusted all judgment to the Son, that all may honor the Son just as they honor the Father. He who does not honor the Son does not honor the Father, who sent him" (John 5: 22-23).

Chapter 19

The Bible Is Not Corrupt...
Says The Quran

It does not take a rocket scientist to conclude that both books cannot be true given the clear contradictions. Here comes the good stuff. This is where my Muslim friends will again say that the Bible is corrupt and has been altered. Why don't they just say that the Bible is entirely false? They can't say that because the Quran actually claims that the Bible was revealed by Allah, as you will see. If the Bible is corrupt, when did that happen—before or after Muhammad? Let's take a closer look.

The Quran itself says that the Bible was revealed by Allah:

...We sent Isa *(Jesus)* the son of Maryam *(Mary)* confirming whatever remained intact from the Taurat in his time, and gave him the Injeel *(Gospel)* wherein was guidance and light...(Sura 5:47).

To Musa *(Moses)* We gave the Book *(Torah)*...(Sura 2:87).

We gave Musa *(Moses)* the Holy Book *(Torah)* and criterion of right and wrong so that you might be rightly guided (Sura 2:53).

We have exalted some prophets above the others and gave Zaboor *(the Psalms)* to Dawood *(David)* (Sura 17:55).

He has revealed to you this Book with the Truth, confirming the scriptures which proceeded it, as He revealed the Taurat

(Torah) and the Injeel *(Gospel)*, before this, as guidance for mankind... (Sura 3:3).

Then in the footsteps of those Prophets, We sent Isa *(Jesus)* the son of Maryam *(Mary)* confirming whatever remained intact from the Taurat in his time, and gave him the Injeel *(Gospel)* wherein was guidance and light corroborating what was revealed in the Taurat... (Sura 5:46).

After them We sent other Rasools, one after the other, and followed them with Isa *(Jesus)* the son of Maryam. We gave him the Injeel *(Gospel)*, and put compassion and mercy into the hearts of his followers (Sura 57:27).

As you can see, it cannot be disputed that the Quran clearly testifies that Allah revealed the Torah, Psalms, Gospel and the Quran. According to the Quran, these make up the message or "reminder"

(*Al-Zikr* as it is called in Arabic) and the Quran says that Allah will guard his message:

> Surely we have revealed this reminder; and We will surely preserve it Ourself (Sura 15:9).

In Sura 21:105 the Torah is referred to as the "reminder," so this term was not just for the Quran. Therefore, Allah must have preserved it as well, so it can't be corrupt. Muslims will say the version we have now is corrupt. Okay, then show me the uncorrupt Torah that Allah preserved. Show me the uncorrupt Psalms or the uncorrupt gospel that Allah gave and preserved if ours is corrupt.

> And to you We have revealed the Book with the truth. It confirms the Scriptures which came before it and stands as guardian over them (Sura 5:48).

The Quran even instructs Muhammad to refer to the Bible:

> If you (Muhammad) are in doubt regarding what We have revealed to you, ask those who have been reading the Book before you (Sura 10:94).

Since the Quran itself testifies that the Bible was revealed by Allah and would be protected by Allah, it cannot be corrupt. If it is corrupt, then either Allah is a liar or he is weak and cannot protect his message.

Furthermore, if the Bible was corrupt before Muhammad, why would he tell Christians and Jews to refer to it over and over? Okay, you say, the Bible was corrupt after Muhammad. How can that be since we have manuscripts that date after Muhammad that say the same thing as manuscripts dated before Muhammad? Maybe the scientists who are dating this stuff are lying? Come on, really? Maybe the Quran is not from God.

Chapter 20

Putting It All Together

In summary, we learned earlier that the Bible we have today is in full agreement with scriptures that date before Muhammad's birth. We can also see that the Quran itself testifies that the Bible was revealed by Allah and that Allah will guard his message. According to the Quran, the Bible could not have been corrupt before or after Muhammad. Even without any further evidence, how can any Muslim say that the Bible is corrupt? That just doesn't make sense. So what are we to conclude from all of this? Let me tell you. The Bible is God's Word and the Quran is nothing more than one man's "revelations" put to work in his quest for leadership and power.

The Quran is a mixture of fact and fiction conceived by a man with human ambitions to conquer and rule. Muhammad's message conveniently tries to appease everyone that he was trying to convert, Jews and Christians. He did this by telling them that he was sent to complete their religion and correct some errors. I don't know if Muhammad was consciously lying or if he actually thought that he was a prophet. Either way, his message is not from God. Can you see how this makes sense? Maybe you should read the Quran and Bible for yourself?

The Judeo-Christian teachings were everywhere during Muhammad's time. He couldn't just come right out and tell these people that they had been tricked by this Jesus. They would have had nothing to do with him. Instead, he led them to believe that he was a continuation of their faith. This made his message much more appealing to the masses. The problem is his message is manmade and it is riddled with error, inaccurate historical information and endless contradiction. Not to mention his ideas about heaven are laced with human lust and fleshly desires. Furthermore, Muhammad's own life was filled with the lust of the flesh as well as the use of the sword. Lust and violence cannot be from God.

I realize that many Muslims and non-believers reading this will find ways to argue the points made; there will be many who don't want to open their minds and hearts to the truth. I can only offer prayer for them. As for Muslims and other non-believers who will open their minds and hearts, the truth is found in the Bible. Go read it and let Jesus speak to you, show Himself to you, and give you salvation and eternal life. Please, don't just follow blindly. Question what you are told; read for yourself. Have you read the Quran or the Bible? Be honest! Come to your own conclusions. Be sure that what you are having *faith* in is worth having *faith* in. If what you are following is true, then you have nothing to fear by questioning it. This also applies to people who think they are Christians because they were born into a Christian family. It doesn't work that way. Each person must accept Christ for themselves. Let's face it—it takes faith to follow any religion. I can't prove who Jesus is. Muslims can't prove that Muhammad's "revelations" are from God. We can debate the Bible and the Quran forever. But at some point, you'll be following something by faith.

So what are you putting your faith in? You either put your faith in the idea that God is saving you from your sin through his work through Jesus, or you put your faith in the idea that you can save yourself from your sin through your work. So, either God is in charge or you are. It's that simple. Can you reach God? NO! Can God reach you? YES! You just have to let God reach you.

Chapter 21

Now What? Tell My Family? Be Disowned?

So I spent all this time gaining all this knowledge, writing this book, now what? It was time to tell my family, but how? Not long after accepting Christ, I told my brother and my youngest sister, and that was a quite a night. It was on a trip to Texas that the opportunity presented itself. I had my brother and sister together and I was ready. . .or so I thought.

I don't recall exactly how I said it, but I'll never forget the next three hours. It was a war of words. As things escalated, I asked Jessica to take the kids upstairs and let me handle it. It would have been too much for them to hear. Plus, I needed someone to be in prayer while this went on and on. My sister was beside herself. She couldn't believe that I'd fallen for this nonsense.

Although it became very clear to me that I knew more about Islam than she did, she continued to defend her faith. Mostly, she defended Islam by rejecting my points with the simple argument that the Bible is corrupt. So my points were not valid anyway. She used this argument almost every time she could not challenge my position. As for Jesus, she just couldn't believe that I thought Jesus was God. How ridiculous could I be? Anyway, you get the point.

As for my brother, he didn't know anything about Islam. He was just born into it, but never lived it. At least my sister was living it to some degree, yet my brother was quick to minimize my conversion and my arguments. However, I could see him distancing himself from the argument as the night went on, as he realized how well versed I was on both religions. Eventually, the night drew late and we had to end our war of words. We agreed to disagree.

Here is the one thing I regret from that night: I spent too much time debating fact from fiction and no time sharing the love of Christ and why they need Him. That's what it's really all about. Over the last few years though, I have had that conversation on more than one occasion with my brother. Circumstances in his life, which I won't share, gave me many opportunities to share the love of Jesus with him. As for my sister, we've had a few discussions, but her mind and heart are not open to Him, yet.

For the next two or three years, we just went on with our lives and didn't discuss the topic much. But we all knew that a time would come that my parents would need to know. They were the only two siblings that I told of the four. Although I suspected that my youngest sister told the other sisters, they did not bring it up when we spoke from time to time. They know now, and it's not a topic that they want to discuss. I love my brother and sisters with all my heart. If nothing else, they know that to be fact. I also love my parents dearly; they know this as well.

I think three or four years passed before I was ready to tell my parents. That's a day I will never forget. I had just finished the first draft of this manuscript and felt that I was prepared to defend my faith in earnest. I also thought that I could convey the love of Jesus to them. I had planned a trip to Texas and told my brother and sister of my intention to tell our parents. My brother was going through some personal issues at that time (unbeknownst to me) so he was not in tune with anything going on. My sister preferred that I not tell them, but she knew it was inevitable.

I told them that my plan was to leave my parents with a package. The package would have a letter and a manuscript. My brother and sister had the manuscript as well. I think they read it. The days before the trip were quite stressful. My wife and I were both very nervous. How would this play out? Would I be in danger? Would I return? Seriously, those were discussions we had. This is a big deal in the Arab culture and in Islam.

We asked everyone to pray for us. The two and a half hour plane ride to Texas was a time to think and ponder how I would muster the courage to do this. I even pondered whether I should do it at all. What's the point? They won't consider Jesus. They're too old to make such a bold move. Satan just kept giving me one reason after another to not do this. Jesus just gave me one reason why I must, because He has instructed me to.

It was on my last night of the visit that it all unfolded. I was saying my goodbyes and was about to head toward the door when my father pulled me aside and said he had something for me. He handed me a plastic bag with a book in it. It was a Quran; I was stunned. He told me to take it home and read the sections he'd marked. In all of my life he had not so much as mentioned a verse from the Quran and this was the day he wanted to give me this? *Really God, today?* I took the bag and told my father that I also had something for him and mom to read. I handed him a large sealed envelope and told him to open it tomorrow. Yes, I took the wimpy road knowing I'd be in San Diego when they opened the package.

The flight back to San Diego was surreal; it was like I was the only one on the plane. I had so much going on in my mind. It was on the plane that I opened the Quran to the pages that my father had marked. I don't recall the exact verses, but I recall the theme. He had marked verses where the Quran praises and honors Jesus. I couldn't believe what I was reading. My father was reaching out to tell me that it's okay that my wife is Christian and that I am Muslim. Everything would be fine. And there was my letter saying the exact opposite. He was reading my words that claimed there can only be one Truth and that was the Jesus of the Bible, making Islam false. Wow! I still can't believe how God orchestrated those events.

I landed in San Diego and my voicemail had some tough messages to listen to. My sister informed me that my parents had disowned me; they considered me dead to them now. My sister said my mother had not stopped crying for hours and my father seemed suicidal. They were devastated. She took my call and I told her I'd be on the next flight back. She said not to bother because they don't want to speak to me again. That was tough to hear. I called my brother and he conveyed the same message. He suggested that I just go away for the time being. I could do nothing now but pray.

The next days, weeks and months were very hard. It was day to day. I would call my sister or brother and they had no good news; they would just say that things were bad. She said both parents cry and sleep a lot. Their health was on the decline. She couldn't believe what I'd done. I could hardly believe it. I knew it *had* to happen though. I just wished there could have been a better way. I don't think there was any other way.

I came to find out that neither of my parents would touch the manuscript. They read the letter and insisted that my brother take and burn the manuscript. Needless to say, the letter was enough. It proclaimed my faith in Jesus. God's plan has not fully played out yet for my family, but I am sure this was part of His plan. His plan will be complete when they accept Jesus as their Savior. I pray that day will come soon.

It took over a year before my parents would consider speaking with me. So there I was on a flight to Texas again. Another two and a half hours to ponder what would happen next. Would they actually speak with me? Was I being set up? Will they have the Imam from the Mosque there to greet me? Would I return? Yes, once again, these questions came up in my mind and Jessica's.

And there I was standing at their front door, terrified. Fortunately, there was no Imam to greet me, just my parents. My sister quickly made herself scarce and left me with them. I don't recall what the first words were. I think my mom was quick to tell me how wrong this was for me to do. My father chimed in, but was not as vocal. Here is where things got interesting. The conversation quickly turned to them insisting that I tell no one else about this. I was not to tell anyone from their family and more importantly, I could never publish this book.

So there it was—their biggest concern was the family reputation. I would think that their biggest concern would be that their son is now doomed to hell for following a false religion and that they'd spend their waking hours trying to show him the error of his ways and turn him back to Islam. That did not happen. In fact, it has never happened. Interesting? So within about an hour my parents were done with this conversation. It was time to sweep this under the rug and move on—so I thought. Apparently, my father was not ready for the conversation to end. There I was on car ride with my father and he shared openly about what he believed and did not believe. The conversation was quite revealing. I'll not share the details. I'll just say it was eye opening.

Where do things stand now? My father has recently decided to separate from my mother and he now lives alone in his home on the West Bank. My mother had no desire to go back and lives in Texas with my sister. My mother prays five times a day and follows Islam to the best of her ability. She and I have a very strong relationship. She knows that I am the one she can count on in times of need. We don't discuss religion though—she just makes it a point to say to me often "Allah Ehdeek". It means that she hopes Allah will settle me down.

As for my father, I am not sure what to say. I just pray for him. I pray for them all. My sister in Texas—our relationship is very strong. It always has been; my brother—he could write two books about his crazy life. I pray for him. My older sisters—we speak from time to time. I pray for them.

Conclusion. . .What About You?

What about you? If you are a Christian and want to reach out to Muslims or any other non-believer, here is the PLAN:

P - <u>Pray</u> for them often.

L - <u>Love</u> them because they are God's children too and have been deceived!

A - <u>Answer</u> their questions and objections—you now have some tools.

N - <u>Never</u> give up. It takes time. Keep repeating the PLAN.

What if you are not a Christian? Now is the time! How can you start a relationship with Christ? It is as simple as ABC:

A - <u>Admit</u> you are like all of us—a sinner who falls short of God's perfect, holy standard.

B - <u>Believe</u> that God became flesh in Jesus and paid the penalty for your sins on the cross and rose in glory on the third day.

C - <u>Confess</u> that Jesus Christ is Lord of your life and walk with Him thereafter.

This was my prayer March 23, 2003 in Dr. David Jeremiah's office:

> "God, I know that I am a sinner and I ask for your forgiveness. I ask to receive Jesus Christ, your Son, into my heart and into my life as my Savior. Let the Holy Spirit guide me from this point forward".

Conclusion. . .What About You?

You can do this right where you are, right now. Just open your heart and talk to Him. God Bless.

If you'd like to contact me please email to:

samabuj@gmail.com

CPSIA information can be obtained
at www.ICGtesting.com
Printed in the USA
FSOW04n2328030516
20011FS